Preface

Throughout the 1930s, Leon Trotsky sought to lead an international fight to combat the rising fascist movement in Europe and its incipient forms in the United States and elsewhere. His writings on the origins and nature of fascism helped arm workers organizations and communist parties to advance a strategy to defeat fascism, overturn the capitalist state, and establish the revolutionary power of the working class. This pamphlet was first published in 1944. It contains excerpts of Trotsky's writings from 1930 until his death in 1940. A second edition was published in 1969. For this printing the text has been scanned and reset.

The full text of the articles reproduced here is available in several books by Trotsky published by Pathfinder, including *The Struggle against Fascism in Germany* and *Leon Trotsky on France*. The source of each excerpt is noted in the first footnote of the item. In cases where more than one consecutive item is taken from the same article, the source is only noted the first time.

● ● ●

Leon Trotsky was a central leader of the October 1917 revolution in Russia. During the Soviet republic's first ten years he served as foreign minister, head of the Red army during the civil war of 1918–20, convener of economic planning bodies, and a leader of the Communist International. Following Lenin's death in 1924, Trotsky was the principal leader of the fight to defend Lenin's revolutionary course against the anti-working-class policies and actions of the growing petty-bourgeois caste whose most prominent spokesperson was Joseph Stalin. He was expelled from the Soviet Union in 1929. In the years that he wrote the selections included in this pamphlet, Trotsky lived first in France and then in Norway, before being deported by the capitalist governments of those countries. He was assassinated in Mexico in 1940 by an agent of Stalin's secret police.

February 1996

Fascism—what is it?

What is fascism?[1] The name originated in Italy. Were all the forms of counterrevolutionary dictatorship fascist or not (that is to say, prior to the advent of fascism in Italy)?

The former dictatorship in Spain of Primo de Rivera, 1923–30, is called a fascist dictatorship by the Comintern.[2] Is this correct or not? We believe that it is incorrect.

The fascist movement in Italy was a spontaneous movement of large masses, with new leaders from the rank and file. It is a plebeian movement in origin, directed and financed by big capitalist powers. It issued forth from the petty bourgeoisie, the slum proletariat, and even to a certain extent from the proletarian masses; Mussolini, a former socialist, is a "self-made" man arising from this movement.

---

1. Extracted from a November 15, 1931, letter to a comrade; printed in the *Militant,* January 16, 1932. For the entire letter see *Writings of Leon Trotsky: Supplement, 1929–33* (New York: Pathfinder, 1979), pp. 99–100.

2. The Comintern, or Communist International, was the world organization of the communist movement founded in 1919 as a revolutionary alternative to the class-collaborationist Socialist (Second) International. By the mid-1920s, however, it had become dominated by a ruling petty-bourgeois caste in the Soviet Union that subordinated the interests of the world working class to defense of its own perks and privileges.

Primo de Rivera was an aristocrat. He occupied a high military and bureaucratic post and was chief governor of Catalonia. He accomplished his overthrow with the aid of state and military forces. The dictatorships of Spain and Italy are two totally different forms of dictatorship. It is necessary to distinguish between them. Mussolini had difficulty in reconciling many old military institutions with the fascist militia. This problem did not exist for Primo de Rivera.

The movement in Germany is analogous mostly to the Italian. It is a mass movement, with its leaders employing a great deal of socialist demagogy. This is necessary for the creation of the mass movement.

The genuine basis (for fascism) is the petty bourgeoisie. In Italy it has a very large base—the petty bourgeoisie of the towns and cities, and the peasantry. In Germany, likewise, there is a large base for fascism. . . .

It may be said, and this is true to a certain extent, that the new middle class, the functionaries of the state, the private administrators, etc., can constitute such a base. But this is a new question that must be analyzed. . . .

In order to be capable of foreseeing anything with regard to fascism, it is necessary to have a definition of that idea. What is fascism? What are its base, its form, and its characteristics? How will its development take place? It is necessary to proceed in a scientific and Marxian manner.

How Mussolini triumphed

At the moment that the "normal" police and military resources of the bourgeois dictatorship, together with their parliamentary screens, no longer suffice to hold society in a state of equilibrium—the turn of the fascist regime arrives.[3] Through the fascist agency, capitalism sets in motion the masses of the crazed petty bourgeoisie and the bands of declassed and demoralized lumpenproletariat—all the countless human beings whom finance capital itself has brought to desperation and frenzy.

From fascism the bourgeoisie demands a thorough job; once it has resorted to methods of civil war, it insists on having peace for a period of years. And the fascist agency, by utilizing the petty bourgeoisie as a battering ram, by overwhelming all obstacles in its path, does a thorough job. After fascism is victorious, finance capital directly and immediately gathers into its hands, as in a vise of steel, all the organs and institutions of sovereignty, the executive, administrative, and educational powers of the state: the entire state apparatus together with the army, the municipalities, the universities, the schools, the press, the trade unions, and the cooperatives. When a state turns fascist, it does not mean only that the forms and methods of government are changed in accordance with the patterns set by Mussolini—the changes in this sphere ultimately play a minor role—but it means first of all for the most part that the workers organizations are annihilated; that the proletariat is reduced to an amorphous state; and that a system of administration is created which penetrates deeply into the masses and which serves to frustrate the independent crystallization of the proletariat. Therein precisely is the gist of fascism. . . .

---

3. From "What Next? Vital Questions for the German Proletariat," January 27, 1932. For the entire article see Leon Trotsky, *The Struggle against Fascism in Germany* (New York: Pathfinder, 1971), pp. 142–257.

* * *

Italian fascism was the immediate outgrowth of the betrayal by the reformists of the uprising of the Italian proletariat. From the time the [first world] war ended, there was an upward trend in the revolutionary movement in Italy, and in September 1920 it resulted in the seizure of factories and industries by the workers. The dictatorship of the proletariat was an actual fact; all that was lacking was to organize it and to draw from it all the necessary conclusions. The social democracy took fright and sprang back. After its bold and heroic exertions, the proletariat was left facing the void. The disruption of the revolutionary movement became the most important factor in the growth of fascism. In September, the revolutionary advance came to a standstill; and November already witnessed the first major demonstration of the fascists (the seizure of Bologna).[4]

True, the proletariat, even after the September catastrophe, was capable of waging defensive battles. But the social democracy was concerned with only one thing: to withdraw the workers from combat at the cost of one concession after another. The social democracy hoped that the docile conduct of the workers would restore the "public

---

4. The fascist campaign of violence began in Bologna, November 21, 1920. When the social democratic councilmen, victorious in the municipal elections, emerged from city hall to present the new mayor, they were fired on by fascists. Ten people were killed and a hundred wounded. The fascists followed up with "punitive expeditions" into the surrounding countryside. Blackshirt "action squadrons," in vehicles supplied by big landowners, took over villages in lightning raids, beating and killing peasant and labor leaders, wrecking the offices of working-class and peasant organizations, and terrorizing the populace. Emboldened by their easy successes, the fascists then launched large-scale attacks in the big cities.

opinion" of the bourgeoisie against the fascists. Moreover, the reformists even banked strongly upon the help of King Victor Emmanuel. To the last hour, they restrained the workers with might and main from giving battle to Mussolini's bands. It availed them nothing. The crown, along with the upper crust of the bourgeoisie, swung over to the side of fascism. Convinced at the last moment that fascism was not to be checked by obedience, the social democrats issued a call to the workers for a general strike. But their proclamation suffered a fiasco. The reformists had dampened the powder so long, in their fear lest it should explode, that when they finally with a trembling hand did apply a burning fuse to it, the powder did not catch.

Two years after its inception, fascism was in power. It entrenched itself thanks to the fact that the first period of its overlordship coincided with a favorable economic conjuncture, which followed the depression of 1921–22. The fascists crushed the retreating proletariat by the onrushing forces of the petty bourgeoisie. But this was not achieved at a single blow. Even after he assumed power, Mussolini proceeded on his course with due caution; he lacked as yet ready-made models. During the first two years, not even the constitution was altered. The fascist government took on the character of a coalition. In the meantime, the fascist bands were busy at work with clubs, knives, and pistols. Only thus was the fascist government created slowly, which meant the complete strangulation of all independent mass organizations.

Mussolini attained this at the cost of bureaucratizing the fascist party itself. After utilizing the onrushing forces of the petty bourgeoisie, fascism strangled it within the vise of the bourgeois state. Mussolini could not have done otherwise, for the disillusionment of the masses he had united was precipitating itself into the most immediate danger ahead. Fascism, become bureaucratic, approaches very closely to other forms of military and police dictatorship. It no longer possesses its former social support. The chief reserve of fascism—the petty bourgeoisie—has been depleted. Only historical inertia enables the fascist government to keep the proletariat in a state of dispersion and helplessness. . . .

In its politics as regards Hitler, the German social democracy has not been able to add a single word: all it does is repeat more ponderously whatever the Italian reformists in their own time performed with greater flights of temperament. The latter explained fascism as a postwar psychosis; the German social democracy sees in it a "Versailles" or crisis psychosis.[5] In both instances the reformists shut their eyes to the organic character of fascism as a mass movement growing out of the collapse of capitalism.

Fearful of the revolutionary mobilization of the workers, the Italian reformists banked all their hopes on the "state." Their slogan was, "Help! Victor Emmanuel, exert pressure!" The German social democracy lacks such a democratic bulwark as a monarch loyal to the constitution. So they must be content with a president—"Help! Hindenburg,[6] exert pressure!"

---

5. The Versailles Treaty was imposed on Germany at the end of World War I. Its most hated feature was the unending tribute to the victorious allies in the form of "reparations" for war damages and losses. The crisis referred to was the economic depression that swept the capitalist world after the Wall Street crash of 1929.

6. Field Marshal Paul von Hindenburg (1847–1934) was a Junker general who gained fame in World War I and later become president of the Weimar Republic. In 1932 the social democrats supported him for reelection as a "lesser evil" to the Nazis. He appointed Hitler chancellor in January 1933.

While waging battle against Mussolini, that is, while retreating before him, Turati[7] let loose his dazzling motto, "One must have the manhood to be a coward." The German reformists are less frisky with their slogans. They demand "Courage under unpopularity" *(Mut zur Unpopularitaet)*— which amounts to the same thing. One must not be afraid of the unpopularity which has been aroused by one's own cowardly temporizing with the enemy.

Identical causes produce identical effects. Were the march of events dependent upon the social democratic party leadership, Hitler's career would be assured.

One must admit, however, that the German Communist Party has also learned little from the Italian experience.

The Italian Communist Party came into being almost simultaneously with fascism. But the same conditions of revolutionary ebb tide, which carried the fascists to power, served to deter the development of the Communist Party. It did not give itself an accounting as to the full sweep of the fascist danger; it lulled itself with revolutionary illusions; it was irreconcilably antagonistic to the policy of the united front; in short, it was stricken with all the infantile diseases. Small wonder! It was only two years old. In its eyes, fascism appeared to be only "capitalist reaction." The *particular* traits of fascism which spring from the mobilization of the petty bourgeoisie against the proletariat, the Communist Party was unable to discern. Italian comrades inform me that, with the sole exception of Gramsci,[8] the Communist Party would not even allow for the possibility

---

7. Filippo Turati (1857–1932) was a leading reformist theoretician of the Italian Socialist Party.

8. Antonio Gramsci (1891–1937) was a founder of the Italian Communist Party. Imprisoned by Mussolini in 1926, he died in prison eleven years later.

of the fascists seizing power. Once the proletarian revolution had suffered defeat, once capitalism had held its ground and the counterrevolution had triumphed, how could there be any further kind of counterrevolutionary upheaval? How could the bourgeoisie rise up against itself! Such was the gist of the political orientation of the Italian Communist Party. Moreover, one must not lose sight of the fact that Italian fascism was then a new phenomenon, just in the process of formation; it would not have been an easy task even for a more experienced party to distinguish its specific traits.

The leadership of the German Communist Party reproduces today almost literally the position from which the Italian Communists took their point of departure: fascism is nothing else but capitalist reaction; from the point of view of the proletariat, the differences between divers types of capitalist reaction are meaningless. This vulgar radicalism is the less excusable because the German party is much older than the Italian was at a corresponding period; in addition, Marxism is enriched now by the tragic experience in Italy. To insist that fascism is already here, or to deny the very possibility of its coming to power, amounts politically to one and the same thing. By ignoring the specific nature of fascism, the will to fight against it inevitably becomes paralyzed.

The brunt of the blame must be borne, of course, by the leadership of the Comintern. Italian Communists above all others were duty-bound to raise their voices in alarm. But Stalin, together with Manuilsky,[9] compelled them to disavow the most important lessons of their own annihilation. We have already observed with what diligent alacrity

9. Dmitri Manuilsky (1883–1959) was secretary of the Comintern from 1928 to 1943.

Ercoli[10] switched over to the position of social fascism, i.e., to the position of passively waiting for the fascist victory in Germany.

The fascist danger looms in Germany

The official press of the Comintern is now depicting the results of the [September 1930] German elections as a prodigious victory of Communism, which places on the order of the day the slogan of a Soviet Germany.[11] The bureaucratic optimists do not want to reflect upon the meaning of the relation of forces which is disclosed by the election statistics. They examine the figure of the increased Communist vote independently of the revolutionary tasks created by the situation and the obstacles it sets up. The Communist Party received around 4,600,000 votes as against 3,300,000 in 1928. From the viewpoint of "normal" parliamentary mechanics, the gain of 1,300,000 votes is considerable, even if we take into consideration the rise in the total number of voters. But the gain of the party pales completely beside the leap of fascism from 800,000 to 6,400,000 votes. Of no less important significance for evaluating the elections is the fact that the social democracy, in spite of substantial

---

10. Ercoli was the pen name in Comintern publications of Palmiro Togliatti (1893–1964), who headed the Italian Communist Party after Gramsci's imprisonment.

11. From "The Turn in the Communist International and the German Situation," September 26, 1930. For the entire article see *Struggle against Fascism*, pp. 55–74.

losses, retained its basic cadres and still received a considerably greater number of workers' votes [8,600,000] than the Communist Party.

Meanwhile, if we should ask ourselves, "What combination of international and domestic circumstances could be capable of turning the working class towards Communism with greater velocity?" we could not find an example of more favorable circumstances for such a turn than the situation in present-day Germany: Young's noose,[12] the economic crisis, the disintegration of the rulers, the crisis of parliamentarism, the terrific self-exposure of the social democracy in power. From the viewpoint of these concrete historical circumstances, the specific gravity of the German Communist Party in the social life of the country, in spite of the gain of 1,300,000 votes, remains proportionately small.

The weakness of the positions of Communism, inextricably bound up with the policy and regime of the Comintern, is revealed more clearly if we compare the present social weight of the Communist Party with those concrete and unpostponable tasks which the present historical circumstances put before it.

It is true that the Communist Party itself did not expect such a gain. But this proves that under the blows of mistakes and defeats, the leadership of the Communist parties has become unused to big aims and perspectives. If yesterday it underestimated its own possibilities, then today it once more underestimates the difficulties. In this way, one danger is multiplied by another.

---

12. The Young Plan was aimed at "facilitating" Germany's payment of reparations to the victors of World War I. It was named for Owen D. Young, an American big businessman who was Agent-General for German Reparations during the 1920s. In the summer of 1929 he was chairman of the conference that adopted his plan. See note 5.

In the meantime, the first characteristic of a really revolutionary party is—to be able to look reality in the face.

◉ ◉ ◉

In order that the social crisis may bring about the proletarian revolution, it is necessary that, besides other conditions, a decisive shift of the petty bourgeois classes occurs in the direction of the proletariat. This gives the proletariat a chance to put itself at the head of the nation as its leader.

The last election revealed—and this is where its principal symptomatic significance lies—a shift in the opposite direction. Under the blow of the crisis, the petty bourgeoisie swung, not in the direction of the proletarian revolution, but in the direction of the most extreme imperialist reaction, pulling behind it considerable sections of the proletariat.

The gigantic growth of National Socialism is an expression of two factors: a deep social crisis, throwing the petty bourgeois masses off balance, and the lack of a revolutionary party that would be regarded by the masses of the people as an acknowledged revolutionary leader. If the Communist Party is the *party of revolutionary hope,* then fascism, as a mass movement, is the *party of counterrevolutionary despair.* When revolutionary hope embraces the whole proletarian mass, it inevitably pulls behind it on the road of revolution considerable and growing sections of the petty bourgeoisie. Precisely in this sphere the election revealed the opposite picture: counterrevolutionary despair embraced the petty bourgeois mass with such a force that it drew behind it many sections of the proletariat. . . .

Fascism in Germany has become a real danger, as an acute expression of the helpless position of the bourgeois regime, the conservative role of the social democracy in this regime, and the accumulated powerlessness of the

Communist Party to abolish it. Whoever denies this is either blind or a braggart. . . .

The danger acquires particular acuteness in connection with the question of the *tempo* of development, which does not depend upon us alone. The malarial character of the political curve revealed by the election speaks for the fact that the tempo of development of the national crisis may turn out to be very speedy. In other words, the course of events in the very near future may resurrect in Germany, on a new historical plane, the old tragic contradiction between the maturity of a revolutionary situation, on the one hand, and the weakness and strategical impotence of the revolutionary party, on the other. This must be said clearly, openly, and, above all, in time.

* * *

From Moscow, the signal has already been given for a policy of bureaucratic prestige which covers up the mistakes of yesterday and prepares tomorrow's by false cries about the new triumph of the line. Monstrously exaggerating the victory of the party, monstrously underestimating the difficulties, interpreting even the success of fascism as a positive factor for the proletarian revolution, *Pravda*[13] nevertheless explains briefly: "The successes of the party should not make us dizzy." The treacherous policy of the Stalinist leadership is true to itself even here. The analysis of the situation is given in the spirit of uncritical ultraleftism. In this way the party is consciously pushed on the road of adventurism. At the same time, Stalin prepares his alibi in advance with the aid of the ritualistic phrase about "dizzi-

---

13. *Pravda* was the newspaper of the Communist Party of the Soviet Union.

ness." It is precisely this policy, shortsighted, unscrupulous, that may ruin the German revolution.

* * *

Can the strength of the conservative resistance of the social democratic workers be calculated beforehand? It cannot. In the light of the events of the past year, this strength seems to be gigantic. But the truth is that what helped most of all to weld together social democracy was the wrong policy of the Communist Party, which found its highest generalization in the absurd theory of social fascism. To measure the real resistance of the social democratic ranks, a different measuring instrument is required, that is, a correct Communist tactic. With this condition—and it is not a small condition—the degree of internal unity of the social democracy can be revealed in a comparatively brief period.

In a different form, what has been said above also applies to fascism: It emanated, aside from the other conditions present, in the tremblings of the Zinoviev-Stalin strategy.[14] What is its force for offensive? What is its stability? Has it reached its culminating point, as the optimists ex-officio [Comintern and Communist Party officials] assure us, or is it only on the first step of the ladder? This cannot be foretold

---

14. Gregory Y. Zinoviev (1883–1936), chairman of the Comintern from 1919 to 1926, joined in a bloc with Joseph Stalin and Lev Kamenev following V.I. Lenin's final illness in early 1923 and his death the following year. The Comintern's line in this period led to a series of defeats and missed opportunities, most notably the calling off of the German revolution of 1923. Zinoviev broke with Stalin in 1926 and joined with the Left Opposition led by Trotsky. After the expulsion of this United Opposition from the party in 1928, Zinoviev capitulated to Stalin and was readmitted to the party. Expelled twice more in the following half decade, he was executed by Stalin in 1936 after "confessing" at the first of the Moscow purge trials.

mechanically. It can be determined only through action. Precisely in regard to fascism, which is a razor in the hands of the class enemy, the wrong policy of the Comintern may produce fatal results in a brief period. On the other hand, a correct policy—not in such a short period, it is true—can undermine the positions of fascism. . . .

If the Communist Party, in spite of the exceptionally favorable circumstances, has proved powerless to seriously shake the structure of the social democracy with the aid of the formula of "social fascism," then real fascism now threatens this structure, no longer with wordy formulas of so-called radicalism, but with the chemical formulas of explosives. No matter how true it is that the social democracy by its whole policy prepared the blossoming of fascism, it is no less true that fascism comes forward as a deadly threat primarily to that same social democracy, all of whose magnificence is inextricably bound with parliamentary-democratic-pacifist forms and methods of government. . . .

The policy of a united front of the workers against fascism flows from this situation. It opens up tremendous possibilities to the Communist Party. A condition for success, however, is the rejection of the theory and practice of "social fascism," the harm of which becomes a positive menace under the present circumstances.

The social crisis will inevitably produce deep cleavages within the social democracy. The radicalization of the masses will affect the social democrats. We will inevitably have to make agreements with the various social democratic organizations and factions against fascism, putting definite conditions in this connection to the leaders, before the eyes of the masses. . . . We must return from the empty official phrase about the united front to the policy of the united front as it was formulated by Lenin and always applied by the Bolsheviks in 1917.

An Aesop fable

A cattle dealer once drove some bulls to the slaughter-house.[15] And the butcher came nigh with his sharp knife.

"Let us close ranks and jack up this executioner on our horns," suggested one of the bulls.

"If you please, in what way is the butcher any worse than the dealer who drove us hither with his cudgel?" replied the bulls, who had received their political education in Manuilsky's institute.[16]

"But we shall be able to attend to the dealer as well afterwards!"

"Nothing doing," replied the bulls, firm in their principles, to the counselor. "You are trying, from the left, to shield our enemies—you are a social-butcher yourself."

And they refused to close ranks.

The German cops and army

In case of actual danger, the social democracy banks not on the "Iron Front"[17] but on the Prussian police. It is reckon-

---

15. This and the following selection are excerpted from "What Next? Vital Questions for the German Proletariat." See *Struggle against Fascism*, pp. 142–257.

16. Manuilsky's institute, i.e., the Comintern.

17. The Iron Front, a bloc between a number of big trade unions and bourgeois "republican" groups, was created by the social democrats toward the end of 1931. Combat groups called the Iron Fist, set up

ing without its host! The fact that the police was originally recruited in large numbers from among social democratic workers is absolutely meaningless. Consciousness is determined by environment even in this instance. The worker who becomes a policeman in the service of the capitalist state is a bourgeois cop, not a worker. Of late years these policemen have had to do much more fighting with revolutionary workers than with Nazi students. Such training does not fail to leave its effects. And above all: every policeman knows that though governments may change, the police remains.

In its New Year's issue, the theoretical organ of the social democracy, *Das Freie Wort* (what a wretched sheet!), prints an article in which the policy of "toleration" is expounded in its highest sense. Hitler, it appears, can never come to power against the police and the Reichswehr [German army]. Now, according to the constitution, the Reichswehr is under the command of the president of the Republic. Therefore fascism, it follows, is not dangerous so long as a president faithful to the constitution remains at the head of the government. Brüning's regime[18] must be supported until the presidential elections so that a constitutional president may then be elected, through an alliance with

---

within the unions and workers' sports organizations, were brought into the Iron Front. However, the Front's first "battle" was to campaign for the reelection of President Hindenburg.

18. Heinrich Brüning (1885–1970) was chancellor from 1930 to 1932. Regular parliamentary government in Germany ended in March 1930. There followed a series of Bonapartist regimes, which ruled not by ordinary parliamentary procedures but by "emergency" decrees. They depended not on the old bourgeois democratic party system but on their command of the police, army, and government bureaucracy. While presenting themselves as political saviors needed to get the country through its crisis, and thus as above class and party, they struck their heaviest blows against the working class, since their real goal was reestablishing capitalist stability.

the parliamentary bourgeoisie; and thereby Hitler's road to power will be blocked for another seven years. . . .

The politicians of reformism, these dexterous wire-pullers, artful intriguers and careerists, expert parliamentary and ministerial machinators, are no sooner thrown out of their habitual sphere by the course of events, no sooner are they placed face to face with momentous contingencies than they reveal themselves to be—there is no milder expression for it—inept boobs.

To rely upon a president is only to rely upon "the government"! Faced with the impending clash between the proletariat and the fascist petty bourgeoisie—two camps which together comprise the crushing majority of the German nation—these Marxists from the *Vorwärts*[19] yelp for the night watchman to come to their aid, "Help! Government, exert pressure!" *(Staat, greif zu!).*

Bourgeoisie, petty bourgeoisie, and proletariat

Any serious analysis of the political situation must take as its point of departure the mutual relations among the three classes: the bourgeoisie, the petty bourgeoisie (including the peasantry), and the proletariat.[20]

The economically powerful big bourgeoisie, in itself, rep-

---

19. *Vorwärts* was the principal newspaper of the German social democracy.

20. From "The Only Road for Germany," September 14, 1932. For the entire article see *Struggle against Fascism*, pp. 272–328.

resents an infinitesimal minority of the nation. To enforce its domination, it must ensure a definite mutual relationship with the petty bourgeoisie and, through its mediation, with the proletariat.

To understand the dialectic of the relationship among the three classes, we must differentiate three historical stages: at the dawn of capitalistic development, when the bourgeoisie required revolutionary methods to solve its tasks; in the period of bloom and maturity of the capitalist regime, when the bourgeoisie endowed its domination with orderly, pacific, conservative, democratic forms; and finally, at the decline of capitalism, when the bourgeoisie is forced to resort to methods of civil war against the proletariat to protect its right of exploitation.

The political programs characteristic of these three stages— *Jacobinism*,[21] reformist *democracy* (social democracy included), and *fascism*—are basically programs of petty bourgeois currents. This fact alone, more than anything else, shows of what tremendous—rather, of what decisive—importance the self-determination of the petty bourgeois masses of the people is for the whole fate of bourgeois society.

Nevertheless, the relationship between the bourgeoisie and its basic social support, the petty bourgeoisie, does not at all rest upon reciprocal confidence and pacific collaboration. In its mass, the petty bourgeoisie is an exploited and disfranchised class. It regards the bourgeoisie with envy and often with hatred. The bourgeoisie, on the other hand, while utilizing the support of the petty bourgeoisie, distrusts the latter, for it very correctly fears its tendency to break down the barriers set up for it from above.

While they were laying out and clearing the road for

---

21. The Jacobins were the revolutionary petty-bourgeois forces in the French Revolution of 1789.

bourgeois development, the Jacobins engaged, at every step, in sharp clashes with the bourgeoisie. They served it in intransigent struggle against it. After they had culminated their limited historical role, the Jacobins fell, for the domination of capital was predetermined.

For a whole series of stages, the bourgeoisie entrenched its power under the form of parliamentary democracy. Even then, not peacefully and not voluntarily. The bourgeoisie was mortally afraid of universal suffrage. But in the last instance, it succeeded, with the aid of a combination of violent measures and concessions, of privations and reforms, in subordinating within the framework of formal democracy not only the petty bourgeoisie but in considerable measure also the proletariat, by means of the new petty bourgeoisie—the labor aristocracy. In August 1914[22] the imperialist bourgeoisie was able, with the means of parliamentary democracy, to lead millions of workers and peasants into the war.

But precisely with the war there begins the distinct decline of capitalism and, above all, of its democratic form of domination. It is now no longer a matter of new reforms and alms, but of cutting down and abolishing the old ones. Therewith the bourgeoisie comes into conflict not only with the institutions of proletarian democracy (trade unions and political parties) but also with parliamentary democracy, within the framework of which arose the labor organizations. Therefore, the campaign against "Marxism" on the one hand and against democratic parliamentarism on the other.

But just as the summits of the liberal bourgeoisie in its

---

22. On August 4, 1914, the German Social Democratic Party representatives in the Reichstag (parliament) voted for the war budget of the imperialist government; on the same day representatives of the French Socialist Party did likewise in the Chamber of Deputies.

time were unable, by their own force alone, to get rid of feudalism, monarchy and the church, so the magnates of finance capital are unable, by *their* force alone, to cope with the proletariat. They need the support of the petty bourgeoisie. For this purpose, it must be whipped up, put on its feet, mobilized, armed. But this method has its dangers. While it makes use of fascism, the bourgeoisie nevertheless fears it. Pilsudski[23] was forced, in May 1926, to save bourgeois society by a *coup d'état* directed against the traditional parties of the Polish bourgeoisie. The matter went so far that the official leader of the Polish Communist Party, Warski,[24] who came over from Rosa Luxemburg[25] not to Lenin but to Stalin, took the *coup d'état* of Pilsudski to be the road of the "revolutionary democratic dictatorship" and called upon the workers to support Pilsudski.

At the session of the Polish Commission of the Executive Committee of the Communist International on July 2, 1926, the author of these lines said on the subject of the events in Poland:

"Taken as a whole, the Pilsudski overthrow is the petty bourgeois, 'plebeian' manner of solving the burning problems of bourgeois society in its state of decomposition and

---

23. Joseph Pilsudski (1876–1935) was a cofounder of the Polish Socialist Party and a leader of its right-wing nationalist faction. He was head of the Polish republic from 1918 to 1923. In 1920, he led the invasion of the Soviet republic. In 1926 he organized a coup d'état and established a fascist dictatorship.

24. A. Warski had supported Polish revolutionary Rosa Luxemburg in several disagreements with the Bolsheviks.

25. Rosa Luxemburg (1871–1919) was a leader of the left wing of the German Social Democratic Party. She and Karl Liebknecht were imprisoned for opposing World War I. A founding member of the German Communist Party in 1918, she was arrested and assassinated during the German revolution of 1919.

decline. We have here already a direct resemblance to Italian fascism.

"These two currents indubitably possess common features: they recruit their shock troops first of all from the petty bourgeoisie; Pilsudski as well as Mussolini worked with extraparliamentary means, with open violence, with the methods of civil war; both were concerned not with the destruction but with the preservation of bourgeois society. While they raised the petty bourgeoisie on its feet, they openly aligned themselves, after the seizure of power, with the big bourgeoisie. Involuntarily, a historical generalization comes up here, recalling the evaluation given by Marx of Jacobinism as the plebeian method of settling accounts with the feudal enemies of the bourgeoisie. . . . That was in the *period of the rise* of the bourgeoisie. Now we must say, in the *period of the decline* of bourgeois society, the bourgeoisie again needs the 'plebeian' method of resolving its no longer progressive but entirely reactionary tasks. In this sense, *fascism is a caricature of Jacobinism.*

"The bourgeoisie is incapable of maintaining itself in power by the means and methods of the parliamentary state created by itself; it needs fascism as a weapon of self-defense, at least in critical instances. Nevertheless, the bourgeoisie does not like the 'plebeian' method of resolving its tasks. It was always hostile to Jacobinism, which cleared the road for the development of bourgeois society with its blood. The fascists are immeasurably closer to the decadent bourgeoisie than the Jacobins were to the rising bourgeoisie. Nevertheless, the sober bourgeoisie does not look very favorably even upon the fascist mode of resolving its tasks, for the concussions, although they are brought forth in the interests of bourgeois society, are linked up with dangers to it. Therefore, the opposition between fascism and the bourgeois parties.

"The big bourgeoisie likes fascism as little as a man with aching molars likes to have his teeth pulled. The sober circles of bourgeois society have followed with misgivings the work of the dentist Pilsudski, but in the last analysis they have become reconciled to the inevitable, though with threats, with horse trades and all sorts of bargaining. Thus the petty bourgeoisie's idol of yesterday becomes transformed into the gendarme of capital."

To this attempt at marking out the historical place of fascism as the political reliever of the social democracy, there was counterposed the theory of social fascism. At first it could appear as a pretentious, blustering, but harmless stupidity. Subsequent events have shown what a pernicious influence the Stalinist theory actually exercised on the entire development of the Communist International.

Does it follow from the historical role of Jacobinism, of democracy, and of fascism that the petty bourgeoisie is condemned to remain a tool in the hands of capital to the end of its days? If things were so, then the dictatorship of the proletariat would be impossible in a number of countries in which the petty bourgeoisie constitutes the majority of the nation and, more than that, it would be rendered extremely difficult in other countries in which the petty bourgeoisie represents an important minority. Fortunately, things are not so. The experience of the Paris Commune[26] first showed, at least within the limits of one city, just as the experience of the October Revolution[27] has shown after it on a much larger scale and over

---

26. The Paris Commune of 1871 was the first attempt to establish a revolutionary government of the toilers. The working people of Paris held the city and administered it from March 18 until May 28, when their resistance was crushed by the French bourgeoisie, working in league with the occupying army of Prussia. In the ensuing terror more than seventeen thousand working people of Paris were massacred.

27. The October Revolution was the Russian revolution of October 25,

an incomparably longer period, that the alliance of the petty bourgeoisie and the big bourgeoisie is not indissoluble. Since the petty bourgeoisie is incapable of an *independent* policy (that is also why the petty bourgeois "democratic dictatorship" is unrealizable), no other choice is left for it than that between the bourgeoisie and the proletariat.

In the epoch of the rise, the growth, and the bloom of capitalism, the petty bourgeoisie, despite acute outbreaks of discontent, generally marched obediently in the capitalist harness. Nor could it do anything else. But under the conditions of capitalist disintegration and of the impasse in the economic situation, the petty bourgeoisie strives, seeks, attempts to tear itself loose from the fetters of the old masters and rulers of society. It is quite capable of linking up its fate with that of the proletariat. For that, only one thing is needed: the petty bourgeoisie must acquire faith in the ability of the proletariat to lead society onto a new road. The proletariat can inspire this faith only by its strength, by the firmness of its actions, by a skillful offensive against the enemy, by the success of its revolutionary policy.

But, woe if the revolutionary party does not measure up to the height of the situation! The daily struggle of the proletariat sharpens the instability of bourgeois society. The strikes and the political disturbances aggravate the economic situation of the country. The petty bourgeoisie could reconcile itself temporarily to the growing privations, if it arrived by experience at the conviction that the proletariat is in a position to lead it onto a new road. But if the revolutionary party, in spite of a class struggle becoming incessantly more accentuated, proves time and again to be incapable of uniting the working class about it, if it

---

1917, by the Julian calendar then in use in Russia. By the Gregorian calendar in use today, the victory occurred on November 7.

vacillates, becomes confused, contradicts itself, then the petty bourgeoisie loses patience and begins to look upon the revolutionary workers as those responsible for its own misery. All the bourgeois parties, including the social democracy, turn its thoughts in this very direction. When the social crisis takes on an intolerable acuteness, a particular party appears on the scene with the direct aim of agitating the petty bourgeoisie to a white heat and of directing its hatred and its despair against the proletariat. In Germany, this historical function is fulfilled by National Socialism (Nazism), a broad current whose ideology is composed of all the putrid vapors of disintegrating bourgeois society.

The collapse of bourgeois democracy

After the war a series of brilliantly victorious revolutions occurred in Russia, Germany, Austria-Hungary, and later in Spain.[28] But it was only in Russia that the proletariat took full power into its hands, expropriated its exploiters, and knew how to create and maintain a workers state. Everywhere else the proletariat, despite its victory, stopped halfway because of the mistakes of its leadership. As a result, power slipped from its hands, shifted from left to right, and fell prey to fascism. In a series of other countries power passed into the hands of a military dictatorship. Nowhere were the parliaments capable of reconciling class contradictions and assuring the peaceful

---

28. This and the two selections that follow are excerpted from "Whither France?" October 1934. For the entire article see *Leon Trotsky on France* (New York: Pathfinder, 1979), pp. 29–62.

development of events. Conflicts were solved arms in hand.

The French people for a long time thought that fascism had nothing whatever to do with them. They had a republic in which all questions were dealt with by the sovereign people through the exercise of universal suffrage. But on February 6, 1934, several thousand fascists and royalists, armed with revolvers, clubs, and razors, imposed upon the country the reactionary government of Doumergue,[29] under whose protection the fascist bands continue to grow and arm themselves. What does tomorrow hold?

Of course in France, as in certain other European countries (England, Belgium, Holland, Switzerland, the Scandinavian countries), there still exist parliaments, elections, democratic liberties, or their remnants. But in all these countries the class struggle is sharpening, just as it did previously in Italy and Germany. Whoever consoles himself with the phrase, "France is not Germany," is hopeless. In all countries the same historic laws operate, the laws of capitalist decline. If the means of production remain in the hands of a small number of capitalists, there is no way out for society. It is condemned to go from crisis to crisis, from need to misery, from bad to worse. In the various countries the decrepitude and disintegration of capitalism are expressed in diverse forms and at unequal rhythms. But the basic features of the process are the same everywhere. The bourgeoisie is leading its society to complete bankruptcy. It is capable of assuring the people neither bread nor peace. This is precisely why it cannot any longer tolerate the democratic order. It is forced to smash the workers by the use of physical violence. The discontent of the workers and peas-

---

29. Gaston Doumergue was the Bonapartist premier of France who succeeded Edouard Daladier. (The Daladier government fell the day after the fascist riots of February 6, 1934.)

ants, however, cannot be brought to an end by the police alone. Moreover, it is often impossible to make the army march against the people. It begins by disintegrating and ends with the passage of a large section of the soldiers over to the people's side. That is why finance capital is obliged to create special armed bands, trained to fight the workers just as certain breeds of dog are trained to hunt game. The historic function of fascism is to smash the working class, destroy its organizations, and stifle political liberties when the capitalists find themselves unable to govern and dominate with the help of democratic machinery.

The fascists find their human material mainly in the petty bourgeoisie. The latter has been entirely ruined by big capital. There is no way out for it in the present social order, but it knows of no other. Its dissatisfaction, indignation, and despair are diverted by the fascists away from big capital and against the workers. It may be said that fascism is the act of placing the petty bourgeoisie at the disposal of its most bitter enemies. In this way big capital ruins the middle classes and then, with the help of hired fascist demagogues, incites the despairing petty bourgeois against the worker. The bourgeois regime can be preserved only by such murderous means as these. For how long? Until it is overthrown by proletarian revolution.

Does the petty bourgeoisie fear revolution?

Parliamentary cretins who consider themselves connoisseurs of the people like to repeat: "One must not frighten the middle classes with revolution. They do not like extremes." In this general form, this affirmation is absolutely false. Naturally, the petty proprietor prefers order so long as business is going well and so long as he hopes that tomorrow it will go better.

But when this hope is lost, he is easily enraged and is ready to give himself over to the most extreme measures. Otherwise, how could he have overthrown the democratic state and brought fascism to power in Italy and Germany? The despairing petty bourgeois sees in fascism, above all, a fighting force against big capital, and believes that, unlike the working-class parties which deal only in words, fascism will use force to establish more "justice." The peasant and the artisan are in their manner realists. They understand that one cannot forego the use of force.

It is false, thrice false, to affirm that the present petty bourgeoisie is not going to the working class parties because it fears "extreme measures." Quite the contrary. The lower petty bourgeoisie, its great masses, only see in the working-class parties parliamentary machines. They do not believe in their strength, nor in their capacity to struggle, nor in their readiness this time to conduct the struggle to the end.

And if this is so, is it worth the trouble to replace the democratic capitalist representatives by their parliamentary confreres on the left? That is how the semi-expropriated, ruined, and discontented proprietor reasons or feels. Without an understanding of this psychology of the peasants, the artisans, the employees, the petty functionaries, etc.—a psychology which flows from the social crisis—it is impossible to elaborate a correct policy. The petty bourgeoisie is economically dependent and politically atomized. That is why it cannot conduct an independent policy. It needs a "leader" who inspires it with confidence. This individual or collective leadership, i.e., a personage or party, can be given to it by one or the other of the fundamental classes—either the big bourgeoisie or the proletariat. Fascism unites and arms the scattered masses. Out of human dust it organizes combat detachments. It thus gives the petty bourgeoisie the illusion of being an independent force. It begins to imagine that it will really command the state. It is not surprising that these illusions and hopes turn the head of the petty bourgeoisie!

But the petty bourgeoisie can also find a leader in the proletariat. This was demonstrated in Russia and partially in Spain. In Italy, in Germany, and in Austria, the petty bourgeoisie gravitated in this direction. But the parties of the proletariat did not rise to their historic task.

To bring the petty bourgeoisie to its side, the proletariat must win its confidence. And for that it must have confidence in its own strength.

It must have a clear program of action and must be ready to struggle for power by all possible means. Tempered by its revolutionary party for a decisive and pitiless struggle, the proletariat says to the peasants and petty bourgeoisie of the cities: "We are struggling for power. Here is our program. We are ready to discuss with you changes in this program. We will employ violence only against big capital and its lackeys, but with you toilers, we desire to conclude an alliance on the basis of a given program." The peasants will understand such language. Only, they must have faith in the capacity of the proletariat to seize power.

But for that it is necessary to purge the united front of all equivocation, of all indecision, of all hollow phrases. It is necessary to understand the situation and to place oneself seriously on the revolutionary road.

The workers militia and its opponents

To struggle, it is necessary to conserve and strengthen the instrument and the means of struggle—organizations, the press, meetings, etc. Fascism [in France] threatens all of that directly and immediately. It is still too weak for the direct struggle for power, but it is strong enough to attempt to beat down the working-class organizations bit by bit, to temper its bands in its attacks, and to spread dismay and lack of confidence in their forces in the ranks of the workers.

Fascism finds unconscious helpers in all those who say that the "physical struggle" is impermissible or hopeless, and demand of Doumergue the disarmament of his fascist guard. Nothing is so dangerous for the proletariat, especially in the present situation, as the sugared poison of false hopes. Nothing increases the insolence of the fascists so much as "flabby pacifism" on the part of the workers organizations. Nothing so destroys the confidence of the middle classes in the working class as temporizing, passivity, and the absence of the will to struggle.

Le Populaire [the Socialist Party newspaper] and especially *l'Humanité* [the Communist Party newspaper] write every day: "The united front is a barrier against fascism"; "the united front will not permit . . ."; "the fascists will not dare"; etc. These are phrases. It is necessary to say squarely to the workers, Socialists, and Communists: Do not allow yourselves to be lulled by the phrases of superficial and irresponsible journalists and orators. It is a question of our heads and the future of socialism. It is not that we deny the importance of the united front. We demanded it when the leaders of both parties were against it. The united front opens up numerous *possibilities,* but nothing more. In itself, the united front decides nothing. Only the struggle of the masses decides. The united front will reveal its value when Communist detachments will come to the help of Socialist detachments and vice versa in the case of an attack by the fascist bands against *Le Populaire* or *l'Humanité*. But for that, proletarian combat detachments must exist and be educated, trained, and armed. And if there is not an organization of defense, i.e., a workers militia, *Le Populaire* and *l'Humanité* will be able to write as many articles as they like on the omnipotence of the united front, but the two papers will find themselves defenseless before the first well-prepared attack of the fascists.

We propose to make a critical study of the "arguments" and the "theories" of the opponents of the workers militia who are very numerous and influential in the two working-class parties.

"We need mass self-defense and not the militia," we are often told. But what is this "mass self-defense" without combat organizations, without specialized cadres, without arms? To give over the defense against fascism to unorganized and unprepared masses left to themselves would be to play a role incomparably lower than the role of Pontius Pilate. To deny the role of the militia is to deny the role of the vanguard. Then why a party? Without the support of the masses, the militia is nothing. But without organized combat detachments, the most heroic masses will be smashed bit by bit by the fascist gangs. It is nonsense to counterpose the militia to self-defense. The militia is an organ of self-defense.

"To call for the organization of a militia," say some opponents who, to be sure, are the least serious and honest, "is to engage in provocation." This is not an argument but an insult. If the necessity for the defense of the workers organizations flows from the whole situation, how then can one not call for the creation of the militia? Perhaps they mean to say that the creation of a militia "provokes" fascist attacks and government repression. In that case, this is an absolutely reactionary argument. Liberalism has always said to the workers that by their class struggle they "provoke" the reaction.

The reformists repeated this accusation against the Marxists, the Mensheviks against the Bolsheviks. These accusations reduced themselves, in the final analysis, to the profound thought that if the oppressed do not balk, the oppressors will not be obliged to beat them. This is the philosophy of Tolstoy and Gandhi but never that of Marx and Lenin. If *l'Humanité* wants hereafter to develop the doctrine of "nonresistance to evil by violence," it should take for its symbol not the hammer and sickle, emblem of the October Revolution, but the pious goat which provides Gandhi with his milk.

"But the arming of the workers is only opportune in a revolutionary situation, which does not yet exist." This profound argument means that the workers must permit themselves to be slaughtered until the situation becomes revolutionary. Those who yesterday preached the "third period"[30] do not want to see what is going on before their eyes. The question of arms itself has come forward only because the "peaceful," "normal," "democratic" situation has given way to a stormy, critical, and unstable situation which can transform itself into a revolutionary as well as a counterrevolutionary situation.

---

30. The Third Period refers to the late 1920s and early 1930s when the Comintern, claiming that the replacement of capitalism by soviets was imminent internationally, advocated ultraleft and adventurist tactics. They refused to collaborate with others in the workers movement to oppose fascism and instead built their own "Red" trade unions in the imperialist countries at the expense of the mass labor movement.

This alternative depends above all on whether the advanced workers will allow themselves to be attacked with impunity and defeated bit by bit or will reply to every blow by two of their own, arousing the courage of the oppressed and uniting them around their banner. A revolutionary situation does not fall from the skies. It takes form with the active participation of the revolutionary class and its party.

The French Stalinists now argue that the militia did not safeguard the German proletariat from defeat. Only yesterday they completely denied any defeat in Germany and asserted that the policy of the German Stalinists was correct from beginning to end. Today they see the entire evil in the German workers militia *(Rote Front).*[31] Thus from one error they fall into a diametrically opposite one no less monstrous. The militia in itself does not settle the question. *A correct policy is necessary.* Meanwhile the policy of Stalinism in Germany ("social fascism is the chief enemy," the split in the trade unions, the flirtation with nationalism, putschism) fatally led to the isolation of the proletarian vanguard and to its shipwreck. With an utterly worthless strategy, no militia could have saved the situation.

It is nonsense to say that in itself the organization of the militia leads to adventures, provokes the enemy, replaces the political struggle by physical struggle, etc. In all these phrases there is nothing but political cowardice.

The militia, as the strong organization of the vanguard, is in fact the surest defense against adventures, against individual terrorism, against bloody spontaneous explosions.

The militia is at the same time the only serious way of reducing to a minimum the civil war that fascism imposes

31. The Rote Front (Red Front) was the Communist Party–dominated militia banned by the social democratic government after the Berlin May Day riots of 1929.

upon the proletariat. Let the workers, despite the absence of a "revolutionary situation," occasionally correct the "papa's son" patriots in their own way, and the recruitment of new fascist bands will become incomparably more difficult.

But here the strategists, tangled in their own reasoning, bring forward against us still more stupefying arguments. We quote textually: "If we reply to the revolver shots of the fascists with other revolver shots," writes *l'Humanité* of October 23 [1934], "we lose sight of the fact that fascism is the product of the capitalist regime and that in fighting against fascism it is the entire system which we face." It is difficult to accumulate in a few lines greater confusion or more errors. It is impossible to defend oneself against the fascists because they are—"a product of the capitalist regime." That means we have to renounce the whole struggle, for all contemporary social evils are "products of the capitalist system."

When the fascists kill a revolutionist or burn down the building of a proletarian newspaper, the workers are to sigh philosophically: "Alas! Murders and arson are products of the capitalist system," and go home with easy consciences. Fatalist prostration is substituted for the militant theory of Marx, to the sole advantage of the class enemy. The ruin of the petty bourgeoisie is, of course, the product of capitalism. The growth of the fascist bands is, in turn, a product of the ruin of the petty bourgeoisie. But on the other hand, the increase in the misery and the revolt of the proletariat are also products of capitalism, and the militia, in its turn, is the product of the sharpening of the class struggle. Why, then, for the "Marxists" of *l'Humanité* are the fascist bands the legitimate product of capitalism and the workers militia the illegitimate product of—the Trotskyists? It is impossible to make head or tail of this.

"We have to deal with the whole system," we are told. How?

Over the heads of human beings? The fascists in the different countries began with their revolvers and ended by destroying the whole "system" of workers organizations. How else to check the armed offensive of the enemy if not by an armed defense in order, in our turn, to go over to the offensive?

L'Humanité now admits defense in words, but only in the form of "mass self-defense." The militia is harmful because, you see, it divides the combat detachments from the masses. But why then are there independent armed detachments among the fascists who are not cut off from the reactionary masses but who, on the contrary, arouse the courage and embolden those masses by their well-organized attacks? Or perhaps the proletarian mass is inferior in combative quality to the declassed petty bourgeoisie?

Hopelessly tangled, *l'Humanité* finally begins to hesitate: it appears that mass self-defense requires the creation of special "self-defense groups." In place of the rejected militia, special groups or detachments are proposed. It would seem at first sight that there is a difference only in the name. Certainly the name proposed by *l'Humanité* means nothing. One can speak of "mass self-defense" but it is impossible to speak of "self-defense groups" since the purpose of the groups is not to defend themselves but the workers organizations. However, it is not, of course, a question of the name. The "self-defense groups," according to *l'Humanité,* must renounce the use of arms in order not to fall into "putschism." These sages treat the working class like an infant who must not be allowed to hold a razor in his hands. Razors, moreover, are the monopoly, as we know, of the *Camelots du Roi,*[32] who are a legitimate "product of capitalism" and

---

32. *Camelots du Roi* were French monarchists grouped around Charles Maurras's newspaper, *Action Française,* which was marked by violent antidemocratic views.

who, with the aid of razors, have overthrown the "system" of democracy. In any case, how are the "self-defense groups" going to defend themselves against the fascist revolvers? "Ideologically," of course. In other words: they can only hide themselves. Not having what they require in their hands, they will have to seek "self-defense" in their feet. And the fascists will in the meanwhile sack the workers organizations with impunity. But if the proletariat suffers a terrible defeat, it will at any rate not have been guilty of "putschism." This fraudulent chatter, parading under the banner of "Bolshevism," arouses only disgust and loathing.

During the "third period" of happy memory, when the strategists of *l'Humanité* were afflicted with barricade delirium, "conquered" the streets every day, and stamped as "social fascist" everyone who did not share their extravagances, we predicted: "The moment these gentlemen burn the tips of their fingers, they will become the worst opportunists." That prediction has now been completely confirmed. At a time when within the Socialist Party the movement in favor of the militia is growing and strengthening, the leaders of the so-called Communist Party run for the hose to cool down the desire of the advanced workers to organize themselves in fighting columns. Could one imagine a more demoralizing or more damning work than this?

In the ranks of the Socialist Party sometimes this objection is heard: "A militia must be formed but there is no need of shouting about it." One can only congratulate comrades who wish to protect the practical side of the business from inquisitive eyes and ears. But it would be much too naive to think that a militia could be created unseen and secretly within four walls. We need tens and later hundreds of thousands of fighters. They will come only if millions of men and women workers, and behind them the peasants, understand the necessity for the militia and create around the volunteers an atmosphere of ardent sympathy and active support. Conspiratorial care can and must envelop only the *technical* aspect of the matter. The *political* campaign must be openly developed, in meetings, factories, in the streets, and on the public squares.

The fundamental cadres of the militia must be the factory workers grouped according to their place of work, known to each other and able to protect their combat detachments against the provocations of enemy agents far more easily and more surely than the most elevated bureaucrats. Conspirative general staffs without an open mobilization of the masses will at the moment of danger remain impotently suspended in midair. Every working-class organization has to plunge into the job. In this question there can be no line of demarcation between the working-class parties and the trade unions. Hand in hand, they must mobilize the masses. The success of the people's militia will then be fully assured.

"But where are the workers going to get arms?" object the sober "realists"—that is to say, frightened philistines—"the enemy has rifles, cannon, tanks, gas, and airplanes. The workers have a few hundred revolvers and pocket knives."

In this objection everything is piled up to frighten the workers. On the one hand, our sages identify the arms of the fascists with the armament of the state. On the other, they turn towards the state and demand that it disarm the fascists. Remarkable logic! In fact their position is false in both cases. In France the fascists are still far from controlling the state. On February 6 they entered into armed conflict with the state police. That is why it is false to speak of cannon and tanks when it is a matter of the *immediate* armed struggle against the fascists. The fascists, of course, are richer than we. It is easier for them to buy arms. But the workers are more numerous, more determined, more devoted when they are conscious of a firm revolutionary leadership.

In addition to other sources, the workers can arm themselves at the expense of the fascists by systematically disarming them.

This is now one of the most serious forms of the struggle against fascism. When workers' arsenals begin to stock up at the expense of the fascist arms depots, the banks and trusts will be more prudent in financing the armament of their murderous guards. It would even be possible in this case—*but in this case only*—that the alarmed authorities would really begin to prevent the arming of the fascists in order not to provide an additional source of arms for the workers. We have known for a long time that only a revolutionary tactic engenders, as a by-product, "reforms" or concessions from the government.

But how to disarm the fascists? Naturally, it is impossible to do so with newspaper articles alone. Fighting squads must be created. An intelligence service must be established. Thousands of informers and friendly helpers will volunteer from all sides when they realize that the business has been seriously undertaken by us. It requires a will to proletarian action.

But the arms of the fascists are of course not the only source. In France there are more than one million organized workers. Generally speaking, this number is small. But it is entirely sufficient to make a beginning in the organization of a workers militia. If the parties and unions armed only a tenth of their members, that would already be a force of 100,000 men. There is no doubt whatever that the number of volunteers who would come forward on the morrow of a "united front" appeal for a workers militia would far exceed that number. The contributions of the parties and unions, collections, and voluntary subscriptions, would within a month or two make it possible to assure the arming of 100,000 to 200,000 working-class fighters. The fascist rabble would immediately sink its tail between its legs. The whole perspective of development would become incomparably more favorable.

To invoke the absence of arms or other objective reasons to explain why no attempt has been made up to now to create a militia, is to fool oneself and others. The principal obstacle—one can say the only obstacle—has its roots in the conservative and passive character of the leaders of the workers organizations. The skeptics who are the leaders do not believe in the strength of the proletariat. They put their hope in all sorts of miracles from above instead of giving a revolutionary outlet to the energies pulsing below. The socialist workers must compel their leaders to pass over immediately to the creation of the workers militia or else give way to younger, fresher forces.

A strike is inconceivable without propaganda and without agitation. It is also inconceivable without pickets who, when they can, use persuasion, but when obliged, use force. The strike is the most elementary form of the class struggle which always combines, in varying proportions, "ideological" methods with physical methods. The struggle against fascism is basically a political struggle which needs a militia just as the strike needs pickets. Basically, the picket is the embryo of the workers militia. He who thinks of renouncing "physical" struggle must renounce all struggle, for the spirit does not live without flesh.

Following the splendid phrase of the great military theoretician Clausewitz, war is the continuation of politics by other means. This definition also fully applies to civil war. Physical struggle is only "another means" of the political struggle. It is impermissible to oppose one to the other since it is impossible to check at will the political struggle when it transforms itself, by force of inner necessity, into a physical struggle.

The duty of a revolutionary party is to foresee in time the inescapability of the transformation of politics into open armed conflict, and with all its forces to prepare for that moment just as the ruling classes are preparing.

The militia detachments for defense against fascism are the first step on the road to the arming of the proletariat, not the last. Our slogan is:

Arm the proletariat and the revolutionary peasants!

The workers militia must in the final analysis embrace all the toilers. To fulfill this program *completely* would be possible only in a workers state into whose hands would pass all the means of production and consequently also all the means of destruction, i.e., all the arms and the factories which produce them.

However, it is impossible to arrive at a workers state with empty hands. Only political invalids like Renaudel[33] can speak of a peaceful, constitutional road to socialism. The constitutional road is cut by trenches held by the fascist bands. There are not a few trenches before us. The bourgeoisie will not hesitate to resort to a dozen *coups d'état,* aided by the police and the army, to prevent the proletariat from coming to power.

A workers socialist state can be created only by a victorious revolution.

Every revolution is prepared by the march of economic and political development, but it is always decided by open armed conflicts between hostile classes. A revolutionary

---

33. Prior to World War I, Pierre Renaudel (1871–1935) was editor of *l'Humanité*. He was a right-wing social patriot during the war. After the fascist riots of February 6, 1934, he joined the Radical Party, the main party of French capitalism.

victory can become possible only as a result of long political agitation, a lengthy period of education, and organization of the masses.

But the armed conflict itself must likewise be prepared long in advance.

The advanced workers must know that they will have to fight and win a struggle to the death. They must reach out for arms, as a guarantee of their emancipation.

The perspective in the United States

The backwardness of the United States working class is only a relative term.[34] In many very important respects it is the most progressive working class of the world, technically and in its standard of living. . . .

The American workers are very combative—as we have seen during the strikes. They have had the most rebellious strikes in the world. What the American worker misses is a spirit of generalization, or analysis, of his class position in society as a whole. This lack of social thinking has its origin in the country's whole history. . . .

About fascism. In all the countries where fascism became victorious, we had, before the growth of fascism and its victory, a wave of radicalism of the masses—of the workers and the poorer peasants and farmers, and of the petty bourgeois class. In Italy, after the war and before 1922, we had

---

34. From "Some Questions on American Problems." For the entire article see *Writings of Leon Trotsky, 1939–40* (New York: Pathfinder, 1973), pp. 331–42.

a revolutionary wave of tremendous dimensions; the state was paralyzed, the police did not exist, the trade unions could do anything they wanted—but there was no party capable of taking the power. As a reaction came fascism.

In Germany the same. We had a revolutionary situation in 1918; the bourgeois class did not even ask to participate in the power. The social democrats paralyzed the revolution. Then the workers tried again in 1922–23–24. This was the time of the bankruptcy of the Communist Party—all of which we have gone into before. Then in 1929–30–31 the German workers began again a new revolutionary wave. There was a tremendous power in the Communists and in the trade unions, but then came the famous policy (on the part of the Stalinist movement) of social fascism, a policy invented to paralyze the working class. Only after these three tremendous waves did fascism become a big movement. There are no exceptions to this rule—fascism comes only when the working class shows complete incapacity to take into its own hands the fate of society.

In the United States you will have the same thing. Already there are fascist elements, and they have, of course, the examples of Italy and Germany. They will, therefore, work in a more rapid tempo. But you also have the examples of other countries. The next historic wave in the United States will be a wave of radicalism of the masses, not fascism. Of course the war can hinder the radicalization for some time, but then it will give to the radicalization a more tremendous tempo and swing.

We must not identify war dictatorship—the dictatorship of the military machine, of the staff, of finance capital—with a fascist dictatorship. For the latter, there is first necessary a feeling of desperation of large masses of the people. When the revolutionary parties betray them, when the vanguard of workers shows its incapacity to lead the people to victory—then the farmers, the small businessmen, the unemployed, the soldiers, etc., become capable of supporting a fascist movement, but only then.

A military dictatorship is purely a bureaucratic institution, reinforced by the military machine and based upon the disorientation of the people and their submission to it. After some time their feelings can change and they can become rebellious against the dictatorship.

Build the revolutionary party!

In every discussion of political topics the question invariably arises: Shall we succeed in creating a strong party for the moment when the crisis comes?[35] Might not fascism anticipate us? Isn't a fascist stage of development inevitable? The successes of fascism easily make people lose all perspective, lead them to forget the actual conditions which made the strengthening and the victory of fascism possible. Yet a clear understanding of these conditions is of especial importance to the workers of the United States. *We may set it down as a historical law: fascism was able to conquer only in those countries where the conservative labor parties prevented the proletariat from utilizing the revolutionary situation and seizing power.* In Germany two revolutionary situations were involved: 1918–1919 and 1923–1924. Even in 1929 a direct struggle for power on the part of the pro-

---

35. From "Bonapartism, Fascism, and War." Trotsky dictated this article shortly before his death in August 1940. For the entire article see *Struggle against Fascism,* pp. 444–52.

letariat was still possible. In all these three cases the social democracy and the Comintern [the Stalinists] criminally and viciously disrupted the conquest of power and thereby placed society in an impasse. Only under these conditions and in this situation did the stormy rise of fascism and its gaining of power prove possible.

* * *

Insofar as the proletariat proves incapable, at a given stage, of conquering power, imperialism begins regulating economic life with its own methods; the fascist party which becomes the state power is the political mechanism. The productive forces are in irreconcilable contradiction not only with private property but also with national state boundaries. Imperialism is the very expression of this contradiction. Imperialist capitalism seeks to solve this contradiction through an extension of boundaries, seizure of new territories, and so on. The totalitarian state, subjecting all aspects of economic, political, and cultural life to finance capital, is the instrument for creating a supernationalist state, an imperialist empire, the rule over continents, the rule over the whole world.

All these traits of fascism we have analyzed, each one by itself and all of them in their totality, to the extent that they became manifest or came to the forefront.

Both theoretical analysis as well as the rich historical experience of the last quarter of a century have demonstrated with equal force that fascism is each time the final link of a specific political cycle composed of the following: the gravest crisis of capitalist society; the growth of the radicalization of the working class; the growth of sympathy toward the working class and a yearning for change on the part of the rural and urban petty bourgeoisie; the extreme confusion of the big bourgeoisie; its cowardly and treacherous maneuvers aimed at avoiding the revolutionary climax; the exhaustion of the proletariat; growing confusion and indifference; the aggravation of the social crisis; the despair of the petty bourgeoisie, its yearning for change; the collective neurosis of the petty bourgeoisie, its readiness to believe in miracles, its readiness for violent measures; the growth of hostility towards the proletariat, which has deceived its expectations. These are the premises for a swift formation of a fascist party and its victory.

It is quite self-evident that the radicalization of the working class in the United States has passed through only its initial phases, almost exclusively in the sphere of the trade union movement (the CIO).[36] The prewar period, and then the war itself, may temporarily interrupt this process of radicalization, especially if a considerable number of workers are absorbed into war industry. But this interruption of the process of radicalization cannot be of a long duration. The second stage of radicalization will assume a more sharply expressive character. The problem of forming an independent labor party will be put on the order of the day. Our transitional demands will gain great popularity. On the other hand, the fascist, reactionary tendencies will withdraw to the background, assuming a defensive position, awaiting a more favorable moment. This is the nearest perspective. No occupation is more completely unworthy than that of speculating whether or not we shall succeed in creating a powerful revolutionary

---

36. A series of explosive labor battles in the early 1930s in the United States forged industry-wide unions. Until then, most labor unions had been organized along narrow, craft lines into the American Federation of Labor (AFL). The Congress of Industrial Organizations (CIO) was the federation of industrial unions. The two federations merged in 1955.

leader-party. Ahead lies a favorable perspective, providing all the justification for revolutionary activism. It is necessary to utilize the opportunities which are opening up and to build the revolutionary party.

THE FIGHT AGAINST FASCISM

THE STRUGGLE AGAINST FASCISM IN GERMANY
Leon Trotsky

> Writing in the heat of struggle against the rising Nazi movement, a central leader of the Russian revolution examines the class roots of fascism and advances a revolutionary strategy to combat it. $32

The Struggle Against Fascism in Germany
by Leon Trotsky
introduction by Ernest Mandel

THE SOCIALIST WORKERS PARTY IN WORLD WAR II
WRITINGS AND SPEECHES, 1940-43
James P. Cannon

> Preparing the communist movement in the United States to stand against the patriotic wave inside the workers movement supporting the imperialist slaughter and to campaign against wartime censorship, repression, and antiunion assaults. $24.95

James P. Cannon
WRITINGS AND SPEECHES, 1940-43
The Socialist Workers Party in World War II

THE JEWISH QUESTION
A MARXIST INTERPRETATION
Abram Leon

> Traces the historical rationalizations of anti-Semitism to the fact that Jews—in the centuries preceding the domination of industrial capitalism— emerged as a "people-class" of merchants and moneylenders. Leon explains why the propertied rulers incite renewed Jew-hatred today. $20

WHAT IS AMERICAN FASCISM?
James P. Cannon and Joseph Hansen

> Analyzing examples from the 20th century—Father Charles Coughlin, Jersey City mayor Frank Hague, and Sen. Joseph McCarthy—this collection looks at the features distinguishing fascist movements and demagogues in the U.S. from the 1930s to today. $8

LEON TROTSKY ON FRANCE

An assessment of the social and economic crisis that shook France in the mid-1930s in the aftermath of Hitler's rise to power in Germany, and a program to unite the working class and exploited peasantry to confront it. $24.95

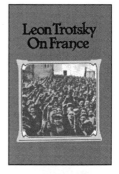

THE FIGHT AGAINST FASCISM IN THE U.S.A.
FORTY YEARS OF STRUGGLE
DESCRIBED BY PARTICIPANTS
James P. Cannon and others

Lessons from the fight against incipient fascist movements since the capitalist crisis and labor radicalization of the 1930s. $8

REVOLUTION AND COUNTER-REVOLUTION IN SPAIN
Felix Morrow

A contemporary account of the revolution and civil war in Spain in the 1930s in which workers and peasants, betrayed by Stalinist, social-democratic, and anarchist misleaderships, went down to defeat under the blows of an armed fascist movement. $23

THE SPANISH REVOLUTION (1931–39)
Leon Trotsky

Analyzes the revolutionary upsurge on the land and in the factories leading to the Spanish civil war and how the Stalinists' course ensured a fascist victory. $31

COUNTER-MOBILIZATION
A STRATEGY TO FIGHT RACIST AND FASCIST ATTACKS
Farrell Dobbs

A discussion on strategy and tactics in the fight against fascist attacks on the labor movement, drawing on the experiences of the Minneapolis Teamsters movement of the 1930s. $8

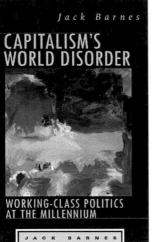

Capitalism's World Disorder
Working-Class Politics at the Millennium
JACK BARNES

The social devastation and financial panic, the coarsening of politics and politics of resentment, the cop brutality and acts of imperialist aggression accelerating around us—all are the product of lawful forces unleashed by capitalism. But the future the propertied classes have in store for us can be changed by the united struggle and selfless action of workers and farmers conscious of their power to transform the world. $25. Also in Spanish and French.

The Changing Face of U.S. Politics
Working-Class Politics and the Trade Unions
JACK BARNES

A handbook for the new generations coming into the factories, mines, and mills, as they react to the uncertain life, ceaseless turmoil, and brutality of capitalism. It shows how millions of working people, as political resistance grows, will revolutionize themselves, their unions and other organizations, and their conditions of life and work. $24. Also in Spanish, French, and Swedish.

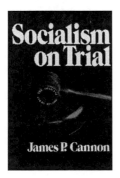

Socialism on Trial
JAMES P. CANNON

The basic ideas of socialism, explained in testimony during the trial of 18 leaders of the Minneapolis Teamsters union and the Socialist Workers Party framed up and imprisoned under the notorious Smith "Gag" Act during World War II. $16. Also in Spanish.

Is Socialist Revolution in the U.S. Possible?
A Necessary Debate
MARY-ALICE WATERS

In two talks, presented as part of a wide-ranging debate at the Venezuela International Book Fairs in 2007 and 2008, Waters explains why a socialist revolution in the United States is possible. Why revolutionary struggles by working people are inevitable, forced upon us by the crisis-driven assaults of the propertied classes. As solidarity grows among a fighting vanguard of working people, the outlines of coming class battles can already be seen. $7. Also in Spanish and French.

Lenin's Final Fight
Speeches and Writings, 1922–23
V.I. LENIN

In the early 1920s Lenin waged a political battle in the leadership of the Communist Party of the USSR to maintain the course that had enabled the workers and peasants to overthrow the tsarist empire, carry out the first successful socialist revolution, and begin building a world communist movement. The issues posed in Lenin's political fight remain at the heart of world politics today. $21. Also in Spanish.

Che Guevara Talks to Young People

In eight talks from 1959 to 1964, the Argentine-born revolutionary challenges youth of Cuba and the world to study, to work, to become disciplined. To join the front lines of struggles, small and large. To politicize their organizations and themselves. To become a different kind of human being as they strive together with working people of all lands to transform the world. $15. Also in Spanish.

To Speak the Truth
Why Washington's 'Cold War' against Cuba Doesn't End
FIDEL CASTRO AND CHE GUEVARA

In historic speeches before the United Nations and UN bodies, Guevara and Castro address the peoples of the world, explaining why the U.S. government so fears the example set by the socialist revolution in Cuba and why Washington's effort to destroy it will fail. $17

Malcolm X Speaks

Speeches from the last year of Malcolm X's life tracing the evolution of his views on racism, capitalism, socialism, political action, and more. $20. Also in Spanish.

Capitalism and the Transformation of Africa
Reports from Equatorial Guinea
MARY-ALICE WATERS, MARTÍN KOPPEL

An account of the transformation of production and class relations in this central African country, as it is drawn deeper into the world market and both a capitalist class and modern proletariat are born. Here also the example of Cuba's socialist revolution comes alive in the collaboration of Cuban volunteer medical brigades helping to transform social conditions. Woven together, the outlines of a future to be fought for today can be seen—a future in which the toilers of Africa have more weight in world politics than ever before. $10. Also in Spanish.

Our History Is Still Being Written
The Story of Three Chinese-Cuban Generals in the Cuban Revolution
Armando Choy, Gustavo Chui, and Moisés Sío Wong talk about the historic place of Chinese immigration to Cuba, as well as more than five decades of revolutionary action and internationalism, from Cuba to Angola and Venezuela today. Through their stories we see the social and political forces that gave birth to the Cuban nation and opened the door to the socialist revolution in the Americas. We see how millions of ordinary men and women changed the course of history, becoming different human beings in the process. $20. Also in Spanish and Chinese.

Cuba and the Coming American Revolution
JACK BARNES

The Cuban Revolution of 1959 had a worldwide political impact, including on workers and youth in the imperialist heartland. As the proletarian-based struggle for Black rights was advancing in the U.S., the social transformation fought for and won by Cuban toilers set an example that socialist revolution is not only necessary—it can be made and defended. Second edition with a new foreword by Mary-Alice Waters. $10. Also in Spanish and French.

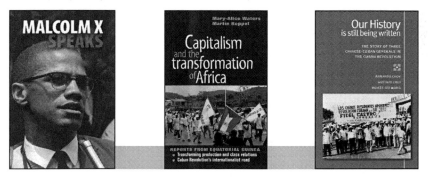

Fighting Racism in World War II
Articles from the Militant
A week-by-week account of the struggle against racism and racial discrimination in the United States from 1939 to 1945, taken from the pages of the socialist newsweekly, the *Militant*. $22

The First and Second Declarations of Havana
Nowhere are the questions of revolutionary strategy that today confront men and women on the front lines of struggles in the Americas addressed with greater truthfulness and clarity than in these two documents, adopted by million-strong assemblies of the Cuban people in 1960 and 1962. These uncompromising indictments of imperialist plunder and "the exploitation of man by man" continue to stand as manifestos of revolutionary struggle by working people the world over. $10. Also in Spanish, French, and Arabic.

Thomas Sankara Speaks
The Burkina Faso Revolution, 1983–87
Colonialism and imperialist domination have left a legacy of hunger, illiteracy, and economic backwardness in Africa. In 1983 the peasants and workers of Burkina Faso established a popular revolutionary government and began to combat the causes of such devastation. Thomas Sankara, who led that struggle, explains the example set for Africa and the world. $24. Also in French.

Feminism and the Marxist Movement
MARY-ALICE WATERS
Since the founding of the modern revolutionary workers movement nearly 150 years ago, Marxists have championed the struggle for women's rights and explained the economic roots in class society of women's oppression. $3.50

How Far We Slaves Have Come!
South Africa and Cuba in Today's World
NELSON MANDELA, FIDEL CASTRO
Speaking together in Cuba in 1991, Mandela and Castro discuss the unique relationship and example of the struggles of the South African and Cuban peoples. $10. Also in Spanish.

New International

A MAGAZINE OF MARXIST POLITICS AND THEORY

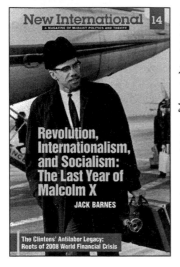

NEW INTERNATIONAL NO. 14

REVOLUTION, INTERNATIONALISM, AND SOCIALISM: THE LAST YEAR OF MALCOLM X

Jack Barnes

"To understand Malcolm's last year is to see how, in the imperialist epoch, revolutionary leadership of the highest political capacity, courage, and integrity converges with communism. That truth has even greater weight today as billions around the world, in city and countryside, from China to Brazil, are being hurled into the modern class struggle by the violent expansion of world capitalism."—Jack Barnes

Issue #14 also includes "The Clintons' Antilabor Legacy: Roots of the 2008 World Financial Crisis"; "The Stewardship of Nature Also Falls to the Working Class: In Defense of Land and Labor" and "Setting the Record Straight on Fascism and World War II." $14

NEW INTERNATIONAL NO. 12

CAPITALISM'S LONG HOT WINTER HAS BEGUN

Jack Barnes

and "Their Transformation and Ours,"
Resolution of the Socialist Workers Party

Today's sharpening interimperialist conflicts are fueled both by the opening stages of what will be decades of economic, financial, and social convulsions and class battles, and by the most far-reaching shift in Washington's military policy and organization since the U.S. buildup toward World War II. Class-struggle-minded working people must face this historic turning point for imperialism, and draw satisfaction from being "in their face" as we chart a revolutionary course to confront it. $16

ALL THESE ISSUES ARE ALSO AVAILABLE IN SPANISH AND MOST IN FRENCH AT
WWW.PATHFINDERPRESS.COM

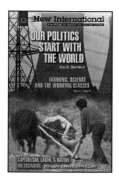

NEW INTERNATIONAL NO. 13
OUR POLITICS START WITH THE WORLD
Jack Barnes

The huge economic and cultural inequalities between imperialist and semicolonial countries, and among classes within almost every country, are produced, reproduced, and accentuated by the workings of capitalism. For vanguard workers to build parties able to lead a successful revolutionary struggle for power in our own countries, says Jack Barnes in the lead article, our activity must be guided by a strategy to close this gap.

Also includes: "Farming, Science, and the Working Classes" *by Steve Clark* and "Capitalism, Labor, and Nature: An Exchange" *by Richard Levins, Steve Clark.* $14

NEW INTERNATIONAL NO. 11
U.S. IMPERIALISM HAS LOST THE COLD WAR
Jack Barnes

Contrary to imperialist expectations at the opening of the 1990s in the wake of the collapse of regimes across Eastern Europe and the USSR claiming to be communist, the workers and farmers there have not been crushed. Nor have capitalist social relations been stabilized. The toilers remain an intractable obstacle to imperialism's advance, one the exploiters will have to confront in class battles and war. $16

NEW INTERNATIONAL NO. 8
CHE GUEVARA, CUBA, AND THE ROAD TO SOCIALISM
Articles by Ernesto Che Guevara, Carlos Rafael Rodríguez, Carlos Tablada, Mary-Alice Waters, Steve Clark, Jack Barnes

Exchanges from the opening years of the Cuban Revolution and today on the political perspectives defended by Guevara as he helped lead working people to advance the transformation of economic and social relations in Cuba. $10

NEW INTERNATIONAL NO. 7
OPENING GUNS OF WORLD WAR III: WASHINGTON'S ASSAULT ON IRAQ
Jack Barnes

The murderous assault on Iraq in 1990–91 heralded increasingly sharp conflicts among imperialist powers, growing instability of international capitalism, and more wars. *Also includes:* "1945: When U.S. Troops said 'No!'" *by Mary-Alice Waters* and "Lessons from the Iran-Iraq War" *by Samad Sharif.* $14

by *KARL MARX and*
FREDERICK ENGELS

The Communist Manifesto *Karl Marx, Frederick Engels*

Founding document of the modern working-class movement, published
in 1848. Explains why communism is not a set of preconceived principles
but the line of march of the working class toward power, "springing from
an existing class struggle, a historical movement going on under our very
eyes." $5. Also in Spanish and Arabic.

Capital *Karl Marx*

Marx explains the workings of the capitalist system and how it produces
the insoluble contradictions that breed class struggle. He demonstrates
the inevitability of the revolutionary transformation of society into one
ruled for the first time by the producing majority: the working class.
Volume 1, $18; volume 2, $15.95; volume 3, $17

Anti-Dühring *Frederick Engels*

Modern socialism is not a doctrine, but a movement of the working class that
arises as one of the social consequences of the establishment of large-scale
capitalist industry. This defense of materialism and the fundamental ideas of
scientific communism explains why. A "handbook for every class-conscious
worker"—V.I. Lenin. In Marx and Engels *Collected Works*, vol. 25, $35

The Poverty of Philosophy *Karl Marx*

Written by the young Marx in collaboration with working-class fighters
in the League of the Just, this polemic against Pierre-Joseph Proudhon's
middle-class socialism gave Marx the opportunity to "develop the basic
features of his new historical and economic outlook," Frederick Engels
notes in his 1884 preface. $9.95